Boredom
BUSTERS!

Activities to Do for Kids Like You!

ISBN 0-439-52312-5

12 11 10 9 8 7 6 5 4 3 2 1   3 4 5 6 7 8/0
Printed in the U.S.A.   40
First printing, May 2003

To Ana Maria and Roberto,

who (sometimes!) let me tag along.

my info

(In case I lose this . . . which
I most definitely won't)

Name: _____

Address: _____
_____
_____

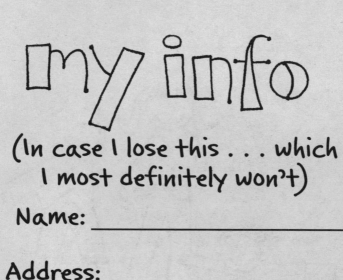

I'll cry if I
lose this V.I.B!
(Very Important
Book)

Boredom
BUSTERS!

Activities to Do for Kids Like You!

by Nancy Mercado

SCHOLASTIC INC.

New York Toronto London Auckland Sydney
Mexico City New Delhi Hong Kong Buenos Aires

Contents

Introduction

Ever feel like summer is the ultimate mixture of good and bad?

Sometimes, summer is

- kicking off your shoes and running straight into the ocean,

- the sound of the ice-cream truck,

- daylight hours stretching out long and luxuriously, and

- having no homework!

Other times, summer is

- feeling desperate for a friend with a pool,

- everyone goes to camp except you,

- getting covered in mosquito bites, and being bored.

Sometimes, summer is magical.
And sometimes, summer just plain stinks.

Yup, it's true. Summer can totally be all of these things. Some summers fly by because there are so many fun things to do. Other summers drag on and make you miserable.

Whatever your summer experiences have been in the past, this will be a completely new one. You have a clean slate. The important thing to remember is that YOU have the power to make your summer great. How? With your attitude and your enthusiasm!

In this book, you'll find ideas for things to do to make your summer better. You can probably think of many more. If you keep your mind wide-open, this summer will be your best one yet!

Chapter 1: Getting Started

Lists help organize thoughts.

Write down three things that you love about summer.

-It's warm outside

-the trampoline is fun

-doing nothing

Now write down three things that you hate about

summer.

-no friends in L.O.A.

-my parents are always busy

-I hate gardening.

Think about the things you love. How can you take advantage of them? Make the most of the best things about the summer! Next to your first list on page 1, write down how you will take advantage of what you love.

For example, your list may look something like this:

Longer days	I am going to get up earlier — I really mean it!
Flowers are in bloom	This summer, I will make a window box full of flowers!

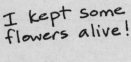 I kept some flowers alive!

That was pretty easy, wasn't it?

Now comes the hard part. Brainstorm some ways that you can improve the things on your hate list. Then, next to your hate list, write down things that will help you overcome what you don't like and make the most of your summer. For example, if you don't like the fact that you don't get to see your friends much during the summer, then imagine some ways that you can keep in touch with everyone. Can you start a postcard pen-pal group?

I spend all of my money.	I'll do odd jobs to make extra cash.
It's too hot!	I will make my own ice cream and ice pops all summer long!

Ask Mega Brain

 Why is it so hot during the summer?

 The sun is stronger in the summer because it's higher in the sky. Its rays are more direct and pass through less atmosphere. This means the rays that reach us are much more concentrated.

 Why do we sweat so much?

 Sweat is the way our body cools itself off. Think of it as our body's own air conditioner. We sweat when our nerves are stimulated (when we are nervous), when it's hot outside (i.e., in the summertime!), and when we exercise.

Chapter 2: Get Out! What to Do in the Great Outdoors

Since so much of the summer is about being outdoors, here are a few suggestions on how to take advantage of all those daylight hours.

Cloud Gazing

Have you ever sat outside on a nice grassy area and stared up at the sky? Seems silly? Just do it! Find a friend and start cloud watching — you'll have a great time. Look carefully at the clouds and let your imagination run wild. What do you see? Is that a rabbit? An elephant? Point out your discovery to your fellow cloud watcher. Can that person see what you see?

Ask Mega Brain

 What are clouds made of?

 You can see clouds everywhere, from your kitchen to your bathroom to outside. A cloud is made of tiny water droplets and/or ice crystals. Fog, mist, steam from boiling water, or your breath when it's cold outside are all examples of clouds.

 Why are clouds white?

A cloud is made of millions of water droplets. When sunlight hits these droplets and reflects off of them, they appear white to our eyes!

Have a Summer Solstice Party

Summer solstice is the longest day of the year because it's the day when we have the most sunlight. In the Northern Hemisphere (the land that lies to the north of the equator), summer solstice is the official first day of summer.

Check your calendar to find the exact date of the summer solstice. It changes every year but is always around June 22. Set your alarm to wake up when the sun does. Spend the entire day outdoors and make some delicious sun tea!

To make sun tea, you'll need:

One-gallon jug

Water

Four tea bags

Ice cubes

Mint (optional)

What to do:

Fill a one-gallon jug with cold tap water until the water is about two inches from the top. Add tea bags. Place the jar in a sunny spot. Let the tea steep (stay there) for three to four hours. Remove the tea bags. Place the jug in the refrigerator to chill for at least two hours. Serve over ice.

Make a Nifty Naturalist Notebook

A naturalist is an expert in the study of vegetable and animal life. A naturalist spends much time outside, exploring and examining the beautiful world. Every naturalist needs a notebook for recording data!

What you'll need:

Several white or colored sheets of paper

One piece of construction paper

Scissors

Ruler

Binder clip

Pencil

Hole punch

Yarn or embroidery thread

One relatively large twig (should be about the length of a notebook)

Large sewing needle

Small twigs from outside

Glue

What to do:

Step One: Determine how big you would like the book to be. Then cut your pieces of paper and construction paper for the cover accordingly. (Remember that because you will need to leave room for the binding on the side, the actual size of the book will be smaller than the paper you select.) Use your ruler for accuracy.

Step Two: Fold all of your sheets of paper in half vertically. Wrap the piece of construction paper around these. Use a binder clip to keep the papers and the cover firmly together.

Step Three: With your pencil, mark a row of evenly spaced dots down the left-hand side of your book. Make sure that they are a half inch from the folded spine.

Step Four: Punch holes where the dots are.

Step Five: Cut a piece of yarn or thread that is at least five times the length of the book.

Step Six: Take the long twig and line it up next to the holes. (You will be sewing around the twig.)

Step Seven: Carefully thread your needle. Starting at the top of the book (and leaving a loose end of a few inches), sew it together by going up through the first hole, down through the second, and so on. Make sure that each time you go through another hole, you are including the twig.

Step Eight: When you get to the last hole on the bottom, start sewing right back up the way you came.

Step Nine: Cut the yarn and tie a knot at the end.

Step Ten: Use the smaller twigs you gathered to make a design on the cover of your notebook. Glue them on with a dab of glue.

Step Eleven: You're done! Now get out there and record some observations in your new notebook!

Play a Game of BOOK TAG!

You've played tag before. This version is different. Get a group of kids together—hopefully, kids who enjoy reading! Find a large area with lots of room to run and lots of spots to hide.

Now pick someone to be IT. The person who is IT counts to 100 while everyone hides. Then IT begins searching for people. The only way a person running can avoid getting caught is if that person yells the name of a book and then crouches down. This buys that person a few seconds, and the person who is IT has to find another person to chase.

Sounds easy? Well, sometimes it's tough to think of the name of a book when you're under pressure! You have to think of it quickly, before IT tags you! (P.S. No cheating and using book series—Animorphs #37 does not count as a title!)

Advice from Super Kid

Super Kid says:

Don't be afraid to ask other kids to play with you. You might find that they are just waiting to be asked. And if you are the one organizing the group, then make sure to ask those kids who might not always get asked. The bigger the group, the better!

Chapter 3: Rainy Day? What to Do Indoors

Sometimes, there are summer days when you just want to lounge around the house or apartment. Some days are so hot that you'll melt if you go outside. This super-sweet treat is so easy to make and is guaranteed to cool you off on days when you are sweating so much you are sliding off the couch.

Make Banana Ice Cream

Cool off with this refreshing, easy-to-make treat!

What you'll need:

Three to four ripe bananas

Freezer bag

Blender or food processor (Make sure you ask a grown-up if you can use the blender or food processor.)

Two bowls

What to do:

Step One: Remove the peels from the bananas and put them in the freezer bag. Put the bag in the freezer overnight or until the bananas are completely frozen.

Step Two: Put the food processor and bowls in the refrigerator to chill for a few hours, or until they feel cold to the touch.

Step Three: Take the bananas out of the freezer and cut them into small pieces.

Step Four: Slowly add the bananas to the blender. (Note: You might want to add an unfrozen banana to help in the blending.) The blended bananas should be smooth, thick, and very creamy—just like ice cream!

Step Five: Pour the banana ice cream into your chilled bowls and enjoy!

Ask Mega Brain

 Where did ice cream come from?

 There are so many rumors about where ice cream originally came from. Some say that in the 1500s, Marco Polo brought the secrets of ice cream with him back to Italy, after traveling in China. Other tales tell of the Roman Emperor Nero, who sent his slaves out to get snow from the faraway mountains and then mix it with fruit and honey. Some believe that the Italians deserve the credit. Other stories say that Charles I from England thought up the recipe. Ice cream is such a yummy treat that everyone wants to claim they invented it!

Make a Piñata!

Whether you're making them or breaking them, piñatas are a surefire way to have a good time!

What you'll need:

An old newspaper

One balloon (as large as you want)

Strong cord or yarn

One large bowl

One cup of flour

Half cup of water

Newspaper cut into two-inch wide strips

Safety pin

Glue

Small pieces of crepe pape

Individually wrapped candies

Masking tape

Two or three streamers

And a few days of patience!

What to do:

Step One: Spread some newspaper on the floor to create a workspace.

Step Two: Inflate the balloon and tie a knot so that the air cannot escape.

Step Three: Tie the balloon with a string and hang it over your workspace.

Step Four: In a bowl, mix together flour and water, making a paste that is as thick as glue.

Step Five: Dip the two-inch wide newspaper strips into the paste and begin covering the balloon with two layers. Do not cover the area near the balloon's knot.

Step Six: (The most important!!) Let the layers dry for a full day.

Step Seven: The next day, make sure the paper feels dry when you touch it. Then add another two layers of newspaper strips dipped in paste. Again, don't put newspaper near the balloon's knot.

Step Eight: Let this dry for one more day.

Step Nine: When the newspaper is completely dry, use a safety pin to pop the balloon. Now you're left with a newspaper shell!

Step Ten: Decorate the piñata by gluing on small pieces of crepe paper. Start at the bottom, layering them over one another all the way to the top.

Step Eleven: Now fill the piñata with individually wrapped candies. Lollipops and bubble gum make great piñata treats!

Step Twelve: With masking tape, cover up the small hole through which you inserted the candy.

Step Thirteen: Glue the streamers to the piñata.

Advice from Super Kid

Super Kid says:

If you don't have all
of these supplies, improvise!
Make the piñata without streamers. Or use paint
and turn your piñata into a famous person. Use your
imagination!

Ask Mega Brain

 Q *What is the history behind piñatas?*

A Piñatas were supposedly seen by Marco Polo (there's that name again!) in China and were used for agricultural ceremonies. Similar ceremonies have been recorded in Africa. Piñatas were also used in Italy for religious ceremonies, then brought by Spanish missionaries to Mexico. Today, the piñata is a fun party game filled with treats!

Try Indoor Camping

When you camp, you sleep outside, usually in a tent. But sometimes, you can't go outside. Why not bring camping indoors? Can you borrow a tent from someone in your family? Can you make your own tent out of chairs and sheets?

Every camping trip needs S'mores. Try this recipe. Make sure you ask for an adult's help when using the stove.

What you'll need:

Graham crackers

Cookie sheet

Tin foil

Chocolate bars

Marshmallows

Sticks

What to do:

Step One: Break the graham crackers in half so that they are square-shaped.

Step Two: Arrange the graham crackers on a cookie sheet covered with tin foil.

Step Three: Put three small pieces of chocolate on each graham cracker. Put the cookie sheet aside.

Step Four: Roast marshmallows over the stovetop.

Step Five: Put one marshmallow on top of each graham cracker with chocolate.

Step Six: Cover each with the other half of the graham cracker, making a sandwich.

Step Seven: Cover the S'mores with tin foil and put them in the oven for two minutes at 200°F so that the chocolate will melt.

Step Eight: Remove the cookie sheet from the oven. (Be sure to wear an oven mitt!) Unwrap the tin foil and enjoy. Make sure to share!

Ask Mega Brain

Q *Where did S'mores come from?*

A No one is exactly sure when S'mores were invented. The recipe for S'mores appeared in the Girl Scout Handbook in 1940. Marshmallows, however, date back to ancient Egypt!

I burnt some
marshmallows!

#1
scout

Make CD locker magnets

Have you ever received CDs in the mail that offer free Internet service? Most everyone gets them. Well, here's an idea on how to use something that usually would go straight into the garbage!

What you'll need:

Old CD

Paint

Markers

Magnetic strips (can be found in any craft store or hardware store)

What to do:

Paint your CD. Perhaps you could design what a CD would look like for your favorite band. Or simply paint a really neat geometric design. When dry, add two magnetic strips to the back. Voilà! You have a cool decoration for your refrigerator or locker.

Ask Mega Brain

How do CDs work?

A A compact disc (CD) is a simple piece of plastic
that can store up to 74 minutes of digital data,
which we hear as music. The surface of the plastic is a
long spiral track of data. Along the track, there are
flat areas and bumps. The CD player shines a laser on
the surface of the CD, which can detect the reflective
areas and the bumps by the amount of laser light they
reflect. The drive converts the reflections into digital
data in order to read the disc.

Chapter 4: Still Bored? Things to Do Anywhere...Very Few Supplies Needed!

Sometimes, the most fun games don't require anything but you, a friend, and maybe paper and a pen. These types of games are great for long car rides, stuffy airplane flights, trips on the subway, or your own backyard!

Try these games... and then make up some of your own!

There are many variations of this game... and they all help to improve your memory! The traditional way of playing A to Z begins with you saying, "I am going on a picnic and I will bring..." Now you must think of a food that begins with A (for example, an apple). Your friend then repeats what you said and adds a food that begins with B (for example, bagels). Then you recite the first two items and add a food that begins with C ("I am bringing apples, bagels, and celery."), and so on, and so on... until you get to Z.

You can also play A to Z with favorite actors ("I am going to the Oscars, and I am going to sit next to Casey Affleck."), favorite writers ("I am going to the bookstore and I'm going to pick up the latest K.A. Applegate."), or favorite bands ("I am going to a concert this summer, and Tori Amos is the headliner.").

In all its variations, you'll find that sometimes it's really hard to think of things, especially for those tough letters!

true or false

This game begins by telling your friend a story. It can be a true story from your past or it can be totally made-up. Either way, the story should be told in the most believable way possible. The only rule is that you need to be in the story somewhere!

When you're finished, your friend must decide if your tale is true or false. Then it's your friend's turn!

It's super-fun to pick the strangest story you know that actually happened and see if you can fool your friend. Or the opposite—make up the most normal story that never happened and see if they fall for it!

make it up!

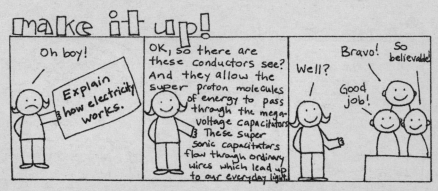

This game is a more complex version of the True or False game. You'll need a pen, paper, and a watch. It is best played in a group, but you can also play with just one other person. Everyone writes five things that they would like someone else to explain or answer. The questions can be:

Scientific: How does electricity work?

Personal: Describe how it felt to get suspended from school.

Historical: Why did the Civil War begin?

Everyday: How do you iron a shirt?

Now put the papers in a hat and choose someone to go first. That person picks a question, reads it, and then takes a moment to think about it. Then that person has one minute to recite an answer. The fun part is that it doesn't need to be the RIGHT answer—the answer must just sound convincing.

The person must speak for a full minute on the topic. Then have that person close his/her eyes while everyone else in the group acts as judges. The group takes a vote on whether or not the person sounded believable. The judges must also consider certain factors, such as whether the person spoke for the entire minute, whether they stammered or tripped over their words, or if they collapsed into laughter!

Someone should keep track of how many "yes" votes each person gets. After everyone has gone at least three times, the game is over and the person with the most votes wins. Of course, if you are having a good time, the game can go on as long as you want it to!

Chapter 5: Closing

Hopefully, this book was a good jumping-off point for you. There are so many possible things to do during the summer. What have you done?

Take inventory and answer the following questions:

I did ☐ all
☐ some
☐ none
of the activities in this book.

I feel ☐ happy
☐ ok
☐ sad
about the way this summer turned out.

The best thing I did this summer was:

_____

_____

_____

The worst thing I did this summer was:

_____

_____

_____

This summer (check all that apply):

Baseball ruled
my summer!

☐

I went to every single
summer movie!

☐

I mastered the art
of rollerblading.
☐

I looked at all the
fluffy clouds.
☐

I wore my bathing suit
every day!

☐

I wrote a million
postcards.

☐